Breaking the Chains:

Understanding and Healing from Narcissistic Abuse

Carolyn stone

Table of contents

Introduction

If it is conceivable, create a scenario or mental image in your head. a member of the family who believes they have discovered their ideal companion, who experiences feelings of adoration, awareness, fear of God, certainty, and engagement. In your capacity as an observer, you are aware that this person is not suitable for your sister. Her accomplice seems to be loving and captivating to her, but in your capacity as an eyewitness, you are aware that he is being dominating.

Suddenly, your friend, who was once vibrant, smart, and astute, is experiencing feelings of trepidation and calmness seemingly out of nowhere. The fact that there are no obvious signs of abuse at all is the most upsetting aspect of narcissistic abuse. Narcissists want to harm your self-esteem and destroy your self-image to boost their self-esteem. Narcissists are often more concerned with what you feel on the inside.

There is a darker side that often remains concealed under layers of manipulation, control, and emotional disturbance in the world that we see, which is characterized by the fact that connections are cherished as the basis of human relationships.

In relationships, narcissistic abuse, which is a phenomenon that cannot be avoided but is commonly misunderstood, undermines the fundamental principles of trust, security, and self-worth. This book, titled "Breaking the Chains: Understanding and Healing from Narcissistic Abuse," makes an effort to shed light on this puzzling and destructive example by providing persons who have experienced the nerve-wracking effects of narcissistic abuse with a few pieces of information, some guidance, and a path toward recovery.

An intentional manipulation that erodes your healthy identity is what constitutes narcissistic abuse. Narcissistic abuse is not merely a clash of personalities or sporadic disharmony within a partnership. The abuser, consistently demonstrating narcissistic features or having a Narcissistic Behavioral condition (NPD), employs a huge variety of techniques to gain control, apply power, and sabotage Your life.

You as the victim is many times naïve and deeply invest resources into the connection, end up snared in a trap of emotional abuse, gaslighting, manipulation, and isolation.

This book seeks to provide You with a far-reaching grasp of narcissistic abuse, looking into its numerous structures and indications. From the inconspicuous symptoms that signify the beginning of manipulation to the considerable influence it has on your psychological, emotional, and at times real prosperity, each part of this complicated dynamic is discussed.

Through this inquiry, You will acquire lucidity on the puzzling mechanics of narcissistic abuse, noticing the red flags that serve as advance notice indications in connections.

Past grasping the ingredients, this book promises to take individuals on a road of healing and rehabilitation. It gives pieces of wisdom into rebuilding damaged self-regard, setting firm limitations, and restoring autonomy and strengthening. Drawing on mental research, authentic experiences, and master guidance, this book presents a path toward recovery, presenting practical approaches and ways for coping with adversity or stress customized to support survivors in discovering the laborious route to emotional freedom.

In addition, "Breaking the Chains" doesn't simply center in on the effect of misuse rather furthermore promotes preventative methods. By offering knowledge of the societal influence of narcissistic abuse and pushing for mindfulness and schooling, this book attempts to encourage individuals to notice, prevent, and protect themselves from succumbing to such damaging relationships.

At least, this book is a promising sign for individuals who have experienced the torment of narcissistic abuse. It fills in as a guiding friend, bringing approbation to their experiences, reestablishing their healthy identity value, and shining a road toward a future emancipated from the bonds of manipulation and control. Through figuring out, mending, and strengthening, this book proposes to supply an exceptional voyage toward an existence of flexibility, self-disclosure, and certifiable association.

Understanding Narcissistic

...Personality Traits

Narcissism, gained from the Greek myth of Narcissus, reflects an excessive self-focus and a grandiose feeling of importance. People with narcissistic personality characteristics typically demonstrate an unavoidable example of behavior depicted by a demand for admiration, a lack of empathy, and a sense of entitlement. Understanding these features necessitates digging into the complexities of the narcissistic range, which envelops a scope of ways of acting and indications.

One of the fundamental aspects of narcissistic personality traits is a distorted sense of self-importance. People expressing such attributes frequently include an inflated sense of their talents, achievements, or position. This gaudiness masks latent instabilities and a fragile self-regard. Their constant need for approval and admiration serves as a defense mechanism to protect their poor self-image, prompting them to continuously seek praise and recognition from others. Another identifying aspect is a lack of empathy. Despite their dazzling outer, narcissist fight to connect with the sensations and experiences of others truly. Empathy, a crucial aspect of good social cooperation, is conspicuously lacking in their interactions. They will typically manipulate situations to fit their own needs, rejecting the opinions and points of view of individuals around them. This deficit of empathy adds to the emotional cost spent upon persons affiliated with egomaniacs.

Narcissistic qualities typically include a preoccupation with thoughts of endless prosperity, power, magnificence, or beauty. They could build a romanticized image of themselves and continuously attempt to keep up with this façade, establishing accounts that promote their successes or distinctiveness. This elevated self-image becomes crucial to their identity, and any threat to this constructed persona is met with defensiveness or hostility.

People with narcissistic qualities exhibit an example of taking advantage of others for self-growth. They could take advantage of connections, exploiting them for their benefit, whether it be emotional, financial, or social. Manipulation and double-dealing become tactics to fulfill their wants without consideration for the consequences on others.

Understanding the development of narcissistic personality features requires consideration of inherited tendencies, environmental factors, and early life experiences. Childhood experiences, including excessive pampering or Neglect, might impact the development of narcissistic tendencies as a survival strategy or as educated behavior.

It's vital to remember that narcissism occurs on a spectrum, extending from solid self-certainty to obsessive narcissistic personality disorder (NPD). While not all persons expressing narcissistic features have NPD, major instances may profoundly hinder relationships and in general functioning, prompting professional mediation.

When a narcissist can no longer control you, they tend to control how other people see you, This deceit will seem uncalled for however stay above it, and think that other individuals will finally learn to know their deceptive techniques as much as you did.

Understanding the features of a narcissistic personality involves accepting the unpredictability of behavior, emotions, and underlying mental aspects. It's a complex spectrum that includes a range of behaviors, from self-confidence to neurotic narcissism. This understanding provides a way to identify and study interactions affected by these traits, ultimately leading to improved partnerships and emotional well-being for both individuals impacted by narcissistic traits and those exhibiting them.

Forms and Manifestations of Narcissistic Abuse

Narcissistic abuse integrates diverse structures and expressions, incurring considerable emotional, mental, and here-and-there bodily injury on You that is related to a narcissistic accomplice. Understanding the many approaches by which this abuse manifests itself is vital in detecting and responding to the damaging influence it might have on You.

1. **Emotional Manipulation and Gaslighting**: Narcissistic abuse typically begins softly with emotional manipulation. Egomaniacs(narcissist) deploy methods like gaslighting, a sort of mental manipulation targeted at making You doubt Your

thoughts, memories, and mental health. Gaslighting means blocking You from understanding reality and making You doubt Your thoughts and judgments. This inconspicuous loss of assurance and self-trust leaves You defenseless and susceptible to the abuser's representation of the actual world.

2. **Idealization, Devaluation, and Discard Cycle**: Narcissistic abuse will in general follow an example known as the romanticizing, devaluation, and discard cycle. At first, the egotist romanticizes You, offering You respect, approbation, and affection. This stage is aimed at gaining Your trust and admiration. Notwithstanding, as the relationship grows, the egomaniac little by bit undermines You, denouncing, undermining, and deprecating

You. This advancement might be dumbfounding for You, leaving them bewildered and emotionally spent. At last, the egotist could forsake You, abruptly breaking off the relationship or withdrawing affection, leaving You feeling abandoned and bankrupt.

3. **Isolation and dominance**: Egomaniacs strive to dominate You by disengaging You from companions, and relatives, and encouraging groups of people. They may decisively undermine Your connections, producing a dependency on the egomaniac for emotional aid. By separating You, the egomaniac takes power, making it tougher for You to go for aid or perspective outside the damaging connection.

4. **Verbal and Emotional Abuse**: Verbal and emotional abuse are prominent kinds of

narcissistic abuse. This combines continual analysis, abuses, humiliation, and emotional manipulation intended to diminish Your self-worth. You could go via regular verbal assaults that work on their assurance and self-esteem.

5. **Financial and Material Exploitation**: now and then, narcissistic abusers could take advantage of Your financial possessions or dominate You financially. This might integrate regulating cash admission, limiting You into financial dependency, or involving assets for coercion and control.

6. **Intimidation and Threats:**Narcissistic abusers could fall back on intimidation methods and threats to maintain control. This may vary from modest intimidation methods, like frightening stares or signals, to clear threats of bodily harm or various

forms of retribution on the off chance that You try to escape or disclose the abuse.

7. **Love-Bombing and Hoovering**: Love-bombing entails bombarding You with undue concern, warmth, and presents to draw you back into the relationship after a period of devaluation or abandonment. Hoovering, then again, is an attempt by the egotist to bring You back into the cycle of abuse after a separation or split, typically with pledges of progress or deceptive displays of regret.

Understanding these patterns and symptoms of narcissistic abuse is crucial in identifying the destructive factors within such relationships. Victims of narcissistic abuse typically pass through essential trauma, fight with their mental health, and encounter challenges in reconstructing their lives post-abuse. Perceiving these instances may assist with searching for help, setting boundaries, and finally breaking free from the cycle of abuse for a healthy and more meaningful existence.

What you need to know about narcissist

We have categories and types of narcissist. The categories include:

Overt and covert narcissism overt and covert narcissism relate to two unique forms of narcissistic tendencies, illustrating various ways persons with Narcissistic Personality Disorder (NPD) may show their behaviors.

Overt Narcissist - Characteristics

Grandiosity: Overt narcissists demonstrate an overt sense of grandiosity.

They freely and confidently brag about their accomplishments, abilities, or superiority.

Attention-Seeking: They aggressively seek attention and praise from others, sometimes dominating discussions or settings to ensure they are the center of emphasis.

Lack of Empathy: Overt narcissists fail to sympathize with others. They may neglect or belittle the sentiments and needs of others around them.

Behavior

Dominance: Overt narcissists tend to be dominant in social contexts, constantly demanding to be in charge and getting continual affirmation.

Exploitation: They exploit relationships for selfish benefit, utilizing people to satisfy their demands without concern for the well-being of other persons.

Covert Narcissist - Characteristics

Insecurity: Covert narcissists, on the other hand, may look more introverted or shy. Their grandiosity is covered by a façade of humility, and they possess deep-seated fears.

Subtle Manipulation: Instead of publicly demanding attention, covert narcissists adopt more subtle kinds of manipulation. They may play the victim or adopt passive-aggressive methods.

Fragile Self-Esteem: Their self-esteem is weak, and they demand frequent reinforcement and adoration, though they may not overtly seek it.

Behavior

Victim Mentality: Covert narcissists typically play the victim, presenting themselves as misunderstood or abused, to elicit sympathy.

Subtle Undermining: They undermine people more surreptitiously, utilizing strategies like gaslighting or subtle criticism to preserve a feeling of control.

While these differences aid in understanding various manifestations of narcissistic tendencies, it's vital to remember that people might demonstrate a combination of both overt and covert qualities.

It's important to note that the study of psychology doesn't categorize narcissists into specific groups. However, certain qualities and patterns are commonly observed, leading to more general classifications based on behavior. Here are the three main categories of narcissists:

Under the categories of narcissism we have different types as well

1. Overt Narcissists

Classic Narcissist: Displays grandiosity, a craving for attention and lack of empathy. They demand attention and praise and tend to dominate social settings.

Somatic Narcissist: Focuses on physical appearance and beauty to get adoration and attention.

Cerebral Narcissist: Prioritizes academic achievement, believing their intelligence makes them superior. Believes intellectual talent is what sets them apart. May disregard feelings as inferior or unimportant.

Spiritual Narcissism: Masks narcissistic traits with spirituality or religious ideas. Uses spiritual jargon to claim superiority and control and May exploit followers in the name of spiritual enlightenment.

2. **Covert Narcissists**

Vulnerable Narcissists: Present a façade of humility but crave constant praise to hide their fragility. Appears meek or reserved but engages in subtle manipulation and plays the victim to undermine others.

3. Malignant Narcissists: Combines narcissistic tendencies with antisocial behavior, including violence, manipulation, and a lack of remorse. Can be emotionally and physically aggressive.

While understanding these categories can be useful in identifying and dealing with narcissistic behavior.

On the off chance that you recognize your accomplice has narcissistic features, you need to know that it is so demanding to be associated with them, You ought to learn how to do the things they can't acknowledge to you. How they may leave you but you are not authorized to depart, most times you are continually hesitant about leaving them because they make you puzzled. You truly desire to glimpse the perfect aspect you noticed when you simply started the partnership with them, now they possess modified you are astonished and bewildered. You couldn't tell whether you ought to abandon them or not because they have found out how to mislead you into accepting it is your insufficiency, they figured out how to project all the blame on you.

"Relationship with a narcissist is held in a place of hope that someday everything will get better without evidence to support it truly showing up."

A broke narcissist would trick you into accepting that what's to come is superb, they would speak about how their ex left them since they were broke so whenever you need to depart you think of that first. It is termed a guilt trip, it is their technique to trap you.

One thing you need to remember about narcissistic folks is that they relish bedlam, regardless of the amount you hunger for serenity they will some way or another need to disrupt that peace specifically when you disagree with them.

"Tips to responding to a narcissist "

Communication with a narcissist can be tricky as it is almost impossible to discourage someone who only sees their own needs and how they can gain from everyone and everything around them. To handle a narcissist, it's important to know how to react to them.

Here are some things you should avoid doing:

1. **Never underestimate them:** It is practically impossible to satisfy a narcissist as they believe they outperform everyone and accept that no one can demonstrate progress over them. They know what to say to achieve what they desire, so be cautious and have a second opinion on whatever they say, especially when it comes to their readiness to change.

2. **Empathy isn't going to happen:** Lack of empathy is one of the key features of a narcissist. They only think of themselves and are selfish. A narcissist cannot offer what they feel, so instead of making them understand this, focus on honoring and

respecting yourself by keeping within your boundaries.

3. **Never give them ammo:** Guard your thoughts, feelings, and other parts of your inner self carefully. Anything you expose to them will be exploited against you.

4. **Don't anticipate their support:** Narcissists have no loyalty towards anybody. If someone doesn't satisfy their requirements or desires, they are put away. Expecting support from someone who only cares about themselves will ultimately harm you.

5. **Never minimize their behavior:** Attempting to get them to feel aware that their actions or words hurt you is pointless as they will ultimately put the responsibility on you. That's why you need to consistently establish your limits, love yourself more,

and value yourself so that you won't be hurt by them.

6. **Don't demand responsibility:** Narcissists could never accept accountability for their actions, so you shouldn't attempt to make them do so. They will continually make you feel like you are the one in the wrong.

7. **Display your best poker face:** Narcissists think everyone is their opponent or target. The closer they get to you, the more they desire to hurt you, shatter your ego, and make you feel like less of a person. Regardless of what they say or do, never give them the satisfaction that they got to you. That is their main goal, so you need to make it uncomplicated for them.

8. **Don't attempt to get even:** Narcissists view everyone and everything as

competition. They offer you compliments and demand further commendations from you. Attempting to get even with someone like them is futile and time-consuming. Just stick to your ideals and be loyal to yourself. Narcissists are exceedingly foolish.

9. **You don't owe them answers or justifications:** Trying to explain or defend yourself is another way to offer them (narcissists) ammunition (details about you). They are not bothered about figuring things out, all they care about is winning.

Here are some things you should do:

1. **Let go of blame:** As you clearly understand, narcissists never accept responsibility for their conduct. They only project blame, so attempting to blame them for their behavior will generate useless

disputes. They believe they are flawless when, in fact, they are the opposite.

2. **Let them believe you are in it together:** If you have ever dealt with a narcissist, you will understand that they use the term "we" not because they care, but because they use it to win your trust. It might be their way of love-bombing you too. So, using "we" when having a conversation with them is a strategy to beat them. Surprisingly, it is also a technique to calm them down and prevent further fights.

3. **Put yourself first:** I don't have to describe how selfish a narcissist is. Remembering to consistently put yourself first will keep you from falling into their trap. Narcissists play mind games a lot, so find out how to put yourself first in any situation with them.

4. **Ignore the bait:** When you face a narcissist, they will attempt to belittle you, make you feel less, and project blame. It is merely their strategy of turning everything on you. Don't fall for it. In this cycle, ignore all their insults (knowing that you are better than what the narcissist claims you are), tune out the bait, and keep focused on the main issue.

5. **It's OK not to receive an apology:** Narcissists never want to admit they are wrong. Therefore, expecting an apology from such a person is a waste of time.

6. **When everything fails, feed their ego:** If you aren't ready to decouple in any of these situations, practice the art of distraction. They enjoy talking about themselves and love to be given a chance to justify that they know more than anyone

else. If shifting the topic doesn't work, try asking for their advice. This is generally the final option to end a dispute with them.

7. **Empathize with their feelings:** You may wonder, "Why should I empathize with them when they cannot do the same for me?" However, empathizing with their feelings can help to diffuse a situation. It doesn't mean you agree with their actions, but it can help to calm them down and prevent further conflict.

Identifying Narcissistic Behavior

Red Flags and Warning Signs

It's important to recognize red flags and warning signs when interacting with narcissistic individuals. These markers can help you identify potentially toxic behavior before it escalates into clear-cut narcissistic abuse. These signs manifest in various behaviors and interactions, providing valuable information about the nature of the relationship.

1. **Excessive Charm and Flattery:** Narcissists often display excessive charm and attraction at the beginning of a relationship. While this can feel genuine, it may be a facade used to gain your trust and control.

2. **A sense of entitlement:** Narcissists have a distorted sense of entitlement. They expect exceptional treatment from you and believe they deserve unwavering consistency with their needs and desires. This can lead to a disregard for boundaries and an assumption that you exist solely to serve their wishes.

3. **Lack of compassion:** A common trait of narcissistic individuals is their lack of genuine empathy. While they may exhibit superficial charm and compassion, they struggle to connect with and understand your emotions. They prioritize their own needs and goals, often without considering your feelings.

4. **Manipulative behavior:** Narcissists are skilled at manipulation. They may use guilt-tripping, gaslighting, or other tactics to

control and manipulate you. This manipulation often starts subtly, making it difficult to recognize until it becomes a pattern.

5. **Constant need for validation:** Narcissistic individuals have an insatiable need for validation and attention. They seek constant praise and affirmation from you to maintain their fragile self-esteem. This can lead to an unhealthy preoccupation with receiving praise and validation for their dominance.

6. **Unpredictable mood swings:** Narcissists may exhibit unexpected mood swings and strong reactions to minor situations. They may fluctuate between idealizing and devaluing you, leaving you always on edge and trying not to trigger negative emotions.

7. **Isolation from support networks:** Narcissists often try to isolate you from friends, family, and other support networks. They may subtly undermine your relationships, creating a dependency on them for emotional support and approval. This isolation makes it harder for you to seek outside perspectives or help.

8. **Boundary violations:** Narcissists struggle to respect boundaries. They may disregard your need for personal space, safety, or emotional autonomy. This can manifest in many ways, from invading personal space to ignoring your emotional needs and opinions.

9. **Blame-shifting:** When faced with responsibility or criticism, narcissists often shift the blame onto others. They refuse to take accountability for their actions and

instead project their flaws onto their partners or external circumstances. This deflects attention from their faults and unfairly places blame on you.

10. **Idealize, devalue, and discard cycle:** In relationships with narcissists, there is often a recurring cycle of idealization, devaluation, and discard. Initially, the narcissist may idealize their partner, showering them with love and admiration. However, over time, they may devalue their partner, criticizing and belittling them. This cycle often ends in discard, when the narcissist abruptly ends the relationship or emotionally withdraws.

Recognizing these warning signs early on can help you evaluate the state of your

to trust your instincts, set and enforce boundaries, seek help from trustworthy sources, and prioritize your own well-being in any relationship. Addressing these warning signs can help prevent the development of toxic dynamics and foster healthier, happier partnerships.

Impact on Victims: Emotional, Psychological, and Physical Effects

Victims of narcissistic abuse go through a distressing encounter that profoundly affects their emotional, mental, and here and there bodily well-being. The treacherous notion of this abuse leaves permanent wounds that permeate various sections of Your life, usually continuing long after the abusive connection has concluded.

1. Emotional Impacts

Uneasiness and worry: victims of narcissistic abuse live in a situation of continuous tension and worry. The capricious thought of the abuser's actions and the worry of vengeance or discipline are still a continual sensation of unrest.

Low Self-Esteem: Continuous belittlement, gaslighting, and emotional control can undermine one's self-worth and confidence, leading to self-doubt and questioning of one's own value.

Depression: The ongoing emotional abuse can have a lasting impact and lead to feelings of bitterness, sadness, and despair. Even after leaving the abusive relationship, it is possible to experience prolonged depression.

Guilt and humiliation: Narcissistic abusers usually transfer responsibility onto You, causing You guilt and humiliation for the abuse You endured so You can feel remorseful about the crumbling connection.

2. Mental Impacts

Trauma and PTSD: Victims typically feel the ill effects of trauma connected with the abuse, provoking side symptoms of Post-Traumatic Stress Disorder (PTSD). Flashbacks, nightmares, hypervigilance, and mental discomfort are common among narcissistic abuse survivors.

Cognitive Dissonance: Conflicting feelings arise from the contrast between the pleasant and the difficult experiences in life. Trust issues can emerge, making it challenging to build new relationships or maintain healthy ones due to the fear of being hurt or betrayed again.

Unable to forgive self: emotions of unworthiness, shame, and guilt disperse after some time they never entirely go. Like PTSD, one minor trigger is sufficient to release the trauma. One additional aspect of this is **hurt self-worth** that causes You not to endeavor to arrive at goals or dreams or

self-damage since You are being made accept that You don't deserve happiness or success.

3. Physical Impacts:

Stress-Related Health Problems: Prolonged exposure to stress and tension due to an abusive relationship might result in numerous medical ailments. You can experience cerebral aches, stomach-associated troubles, impaired insusceptible capacity, and other stress-connected health problems.

Sleep Disturbances: Emotional strain and heightened worry usually lead to unpleasant sleep patterns, like sleep deprivation or nightmares, impacting Your casualty overall well-being and feeding other health difficulties.

The collective effect of narcissistic abuse on You is enormous, It impacts Your mental health, emotional strength, and physical well-being. Perceiving these effects is crucial in supplying aid, affirmation, and particular treatment to assist You with exploring Your healing path toward regaining emotional harmony and rebuilding Your lifestyle freed from the trauma of abuse.

It is important to understand the intricate dynamics of narcissistic relationships, which involve deception, control, and emotional conflict. Recognizing these patterns can help identify the sophisticated web woven by the narcissist to maintain power within the relationship.

The idealization phase marks the beginning of many narcissistic interactions, during which the narcissist shows camaraderie, charm, and adoration towards their partner. This phase is designed to emotionally trap the partner and establish the narcissist's control.

The idealization phase is then followed by the devaluation phase, during which the once-worshipped partner is suddenly undermined and devalued by the narcissist, who becomes critical, egotistical, and emotionally abusive. The narcissist may use tactics such as gaslighting, manipulation, and verbal assaults to erode the partner's self-esteem, creating a sense of dependence and confusion.

After the devaluation phase, the narcissist may suddenly break off the relationship or withdraw emotionally, leaving the partner heartbroken and vulnerable. This sets up a power dynamic that leaves the partner in emotional turmoil, often seeking closure or affirmation from the narcissistic partner.

Alternatively, the narcissist may engage in hoovering, which involves attempting to reconnect with the partner following the dispose of stage. This cycle of idealization, devaluation, and disposal perpetuates a chaotic relationship dynamic, leaving the partner trapped in a pattern of trust and unhappiness.

Control and manipulation are central to narcissistic relationships, with the narcissist constantly seeking to maintain power over their partner. This can involve techniques such as gaslighting, emotional blackmail, guilt-tripping, and isolating the partner from emotional support networks. As a result, the partner's autonomy and self-worth are eroded, while the narcissist's power is reinforced.

A common characteristic of narcissistic relationships is the lack of empathy and emotional intimacy from the narcissistic partner. They are unable to fully understand or relate to their partner's feelings, as they are solely focused on their own needs, goals, and self-image.

Understanding these patterns is crucial for individuals trapped in narcissistic relationships. Recognizing instances of manipulation, control, and emotional abuse can help break the cycle, set boundaries, seek help, and ultimately embark on a path towards recovery and regaining autonomy and prosperity.

Healing and recovery from narcissistic abuse are mind-boggling procedures that involve considerable self-reflection, self-compassion, and committed attempts toward recreating Your emotional well-being. Perceiving the necessity for change is the critical first step on Your road toward healing from the pain created by a narcissistic relationship. In this approach, adopting self-care procedures and survival skills becomes crucial in regaining autonomy, rebuilding self-worth, and cultivating emotional flexibility.

Breaking away from the pattern of narcissistic abuse entails realizing the adverse influence of the connection on Your psychic, emotional, and in some circumstances actual wellness. Recognizing the necessity for change involves:

Validation of Experiences: Validating Your experience as real abuse and acknowledging the emotional toll inflicted by Your narcissistic emotional abuse, manipulation and gaslighting.

Acceptance and Shift in Perspective: Accepting that the relationship was damaging and realizing that the duty regarding the abuse falls completely with the abuser(Your partner), not You. Shifting the attitude from self-blame to self-compassion is crucial in commencing the healing mechanism.

Setting boundaries: Establish boundaries to safeguard Yourself from more damage. This means restricting or breaking off contact with Your narcissistic spouse, maintaining a healthy emotional distance, and prioritizing Your success.

When the acceptance stage begins the healing process, implementing self-care systems and techniques of coping with hardship or stress becomes fundamental for overcomers of narcissistic abuse:

Looking for Help and Therapy: Taking part in therapy, whether individual directing or support gathers, provides a secure area to address Your feelings, gain approbation, and establish ways for coping with stress under the direction of a licensed expert.

Self-Reflection and Journaling: Reflecting on Your feelings, contemplations, and experiences via writing cultivates self-mindfulness and assists with the managing of nuanced emotions originating from the abusive relationship.

Care and Establishing Methods: Rehearsing care, contemplation, or developing practices supports You with restoring a sense of present, establishing them right now, and alleviating tension brought off by prior damage.

Rebuilding Self-Worth: Participating in exercises that boost Your self-worth and self-compassion, such as self-affirmations, self-care traditions, and searching after side hobbies or interests, promotes rebuilding a positive self-picture.

Healthy Boundaries and Assertiveness: Figuring out how to establish and keep up with healthy limitations in relationships and practice assertiveness in correspondence engages You to safeguard Yourself from future maltreatment.

Physical Health: Focusing on Your physical health via typical movement, wholesome eating patterns, enough sleep, and unwinding practices adds substantially to Your overall prosperity and emotional resilience.

Restricting Triggers and Laying out Safety: Avoiding triggers that bring up agonizing memories or feelings linked with the abusive relationship, and building a secure atmosphere that fosters Your emotional recovery and stability.

Tolerance and Self-Compassion: Embracing perseverance and offering Yourself compassion all through the healing process is crucial. Recovery from narcissistic abuse is a path that involves considerable investment, and being nice to Yourself throughout this time is vital.

Healing and recovery from narcissistic abuse involve a multi-layered method involving self-reflection, self-compassion, and devoted initiatives toward rebuilding Your emotional prosperity. Perceiving the requirement for change is the critical beginning stage, trailed by the implementation of self-care methodologies and strategies for dealing with difficult times that promote healing, reestablish Your

self-worth, and encourage resilience in You
as an overcomer of narcissistic abuse

"It is OK to express yourself, oppose rudeness. it doesn't make you hostile You are merely consenting to healthy boundaries."

Breaking free from a narcissistic companion demands enormous strength, crucial preparation, and an inflexible duty to regain Your independence and success. Freeing Yourself from the pull of a narcissistic relationship involves a well-designed process that focuses on Your security, strengthening, and emotional healing. Executing clear strategies is vital for those wishing to break away from the damaging cycle of narcissistic abuse and restore control of their life.

Having knowledge of Narcissistic Abuse: Acquiring a thorough grasp of narcissistic abuse is fundamental to constructing a break-free strategy. Perceiving the manipulative methods, emotional pressure, and instances of control employed by Your narcissistic spouse is vital in authenticating Your interactions and building the mental fortitude to start change.

2. **Building a Support Organization**: Making a strong support network comprised of believed companions, relatives, support gatherings, or emotional well-being specialists is vital. Establishing relationships with individuals who provide acceptance, compassion, and down-to-earth support fortifies Your objective and offers key assets throughout Your shift phase.

3. **Security Planning:**Prioritizing wellness is vital when You are intending to break loose from your narcissistic relationship. Fostering a well-being strategy that integrates collecting your basic reports (ID,

bank records), recognizing secure regions, and building crisis contacts guarantees preparedness in the event of higher hazards or dangers.

4. **Separation and Setting Boundaries**:Gradual distancing and creating strong limitations with Your narcissistic spouse are key stages toward restoring your independence. Restricting or deleting touch, imparting limits plainly, and rejecting to take part in manipulative connections enhance Your aim and debilitate the egotist's power.

5. **Establishing Financial Independence**:Financial independence is crucial in breaking away from a narcissistic partner's financial grip. Make a distinct ledger, safeguard your financial assets, and hunt for genuine advice or support with

money concerns to empower yourself and minimize dependency on your narcissistic spouse.

6. Seeking Professional assistance: Dealing with a narcissistic spouse produces depression, heartbreak, and shock... .. thus engaging with advisors, advocates, or juridical specialists represents great expertise in domestic abuse and narcissistic connections and supplies vital guidance and assistance. You need to Look for expert aid with understanding the lawful repercussions, acquiring defense orders if required, and exploring the emotional nuances of the division.

7. Documenting Evidence: Documenting damaging events, including SMS, messages, or journaling experiences of abuse, may work as fundamental evidence in legal proceedings or when you are seeking protective orders. Documenting relationships with your narcissistic spouse aids in verifying claims and confirming your interactions.

8. **Self-Care and Emotional Recovery:** Prioritizing your self-care and emotional mending is important throughout the approach connected with breaking free. Taking part in activities that increase prosperity, rehearsing care, obtaining restorative support, and nurturing self-compassion aid in addressing damage and recovering emotional flexibility.

"Remember to continuously love yourself as no one will love you better than you love yourself"

Loving yourself more can aid you in moving beyond your narcissistic relationship by prioritizing yourself and caring for yourself.

9. **Embracing a New Chapter:**Reframing the story and embracing the prospect of a fresh start is crucial. Zeroing focus on your self-improvement, rediscovering hobbies and interests, and visualizing a day-to-day living emancipated from the poison of the narcissistic relationship builds trust and stimulates you to embrace a more hopeful time to come.

10. **Staying Committed to Boundaries:**Maintaining solid boundaries even after the split is crucial. Perceiving anticipated attempts by the narcissistic spouse to hoover or manipulate, and maintaining unfaltering enforcing boundaries, guards against backslides into the damaging cycle.

It is tough enough to end a toxic relationship with a narcissist, but packing up and leaving that person will be one of the most difficult choices you will ever have to make. However, at the same time, it will be one of the greatest and healthiest decisions you have ever made. The act of leaving a narcissist may seem to be difficult, or let's just say that it is difficult. However, I assure you that the minute you can break away, you will find that your life is much more peaceful without the presence of your narcissistic former partner.

"You can't force someone to respect you but you can refuse to be disrespected"

You may be pondering significant issues in your thoughts about whether or not you are making the appropriate choice. Additionally, if there is a kid involved, you could have a second thought about leaving the situation.

It is in the nature of a narcissist to trap their partner with a kid, I want you to become aware of this fact.

In this particular case, the most important question that you should ask yourself is whether or not your kid wants to continue to see harmful and abusive conduct directed against you. Secondly, do you want your kid to have the same characteristics as your partner? I guess that you should respond with a NO.

First, there are a few things that you should keep in mind before we remind you of the reasons why you would be better off without them.

What if I offer them a chance to change? The reality is you can never change a narcissist no matter how you try. Some other things may be accomplished but reforming a narcissist is difficult since they see nothing wrong in their conduct, they project blame and the more you remain in the relationship the more terrible they treat you.

What if they are attempting to contact me? You know narcissist leaves you as part of their manipulative methods, they leave you to get power so when they notice that you are not calling them back or pursuing them. They come to win, they don't want to lose. So they contact you back to seize control and attempt to win. hence you have to apply the no contact rule, delete and block their phone, and block them on every social media.

How to co-parent with a narcissist? This a challenging question that a therapist may be asked to deal with both parents. Co-parenting with a narcissistic ex after leaving means establishing clear boundaries, emphasizing children's prosperity, and limiting direct contact. Look for help from friends, family, or experts, prioritize taking care of oneself, and retain documentation for efficient communication.

How can I prevent my kid from being affected or influenced by my narcissistic spouse or narcissist in general? Whoever the person is either a teacher, friend, or parent, children are heavily impacted by others around them, they are too young to be able to tell right from wrong. Children copy folks around them particularly parents that is the reason it is recommended to be on your best behavior around your children and observe the surroundings they are in. Communicate with your kid often as much as they cannot differentiate right from wrong they can still listen and copy what you do and in the case of the other parent being a narcissist you need to strive to prevent too much direct contact between your kid and your narcissistic spouse. Also, recollect children are not things to fight over so you should seek help from a legal practitioner to ensure you acquire custody of your kid to prevent your youngster from suffering abuse.

What to do if your narcissistic spouse obtains custody of your child? This is hard to believe but it could happen, All you can do as the estranged parent is to make sure that the kid is not being manipulated, used to harm you, or mistreated. Always remind yourself that the situation isn't your fault and strive to live the best life you can. Keep the channel of communication with your kid open, and listen with empathy when you communicate with them. This is something they may not be getting from the other caregiver. By no means should to endure being mistreated or insulted by your kid and you should tell them you wouldn't accept that as well because it could be your narcissistic partner manipulating your child. Make careful to prioritize taking care of yourself and constantly tell your kid how much you love them.

Dealing with a narcissist isn't just about placing the blame on them, it is also about dealing with the sentiments that led you close to them first. Also, recollect the part of you that was pushed to the side throughout the relationship.

It is crucial at this stage to remind yourself of all the whys for quitting that relationship. And since that individual doesn't aim to make leaving simple, I want to know you are stronger than you think. Not every individual in the same situation will follow their instincts, stand solid behind their boundaries, and move on. In addition to that, the following are many notable things you need to ensure that you move on completely and safely

No more chances: You believe a person who treated you unworthy of being with them could have no trouble letting you go? If narcissists can no longer dominate you, they will go so what is the essence of giving them further chances? To allow them to make you feel to a lesser degree a human again? Narcissists might seek to come back into your life again, love bomb you, vow to make a difference, and finally whenever you give them another opportunity they abuse it

Don't tell them you are going immediately away: This may seem to contradict what has been mentioned previously but not letting an abuser know when you are leaving may be a sensible move. In an optimal situation, departing when they aren't aware of it will ease a lot of turmoil. A narcissist would do whatever to make you remain It has been said before narcissists wouldn't let you leave them but they can walk out on you at any moment they desire thus leaving without giving them the precise time and day is the best to do.

Don't give them a chance to snoop on you: This goes beyond updating your passwords for all your gadgets. You have to make sure they can't monitor where you are or what you are doing. Log out of everything, create another email account, and make sure you don't possess any type of tracker on your phone. After leaving them go follow the no contact rule(block and delete their phone number, block them on each social network)

Change your bank account:if you at any time revealed your bank data to your narcissistic spouse, it is preferable to change your bank account since a narcissist will do everything to make sure you don't succeed.

They appreciate it when you depend upon them financially

Reconnect with family and friends: Narcissists never allow them since they wouldn't want anyone to offer you advice about them, they don't want you to break loose from them thus they essentially don't want anybody near you. This reminds me of when I was still with my narcissistic spouse he asked me whether I speak about my relationship with anybody, and I answered no since I am not the sort of person to talk about my life with anyone. I didn't realize it was due to the way narcissistic people are. Talking about your personal life with folks may either benefit or hurt you but reuniting beloved friends and family around you is always encouraged.

Once you leave don't return under any condition: Ending an abusive right is equivalent to quitting a habit according to the brain. Think of a narcissistic spouse as a terrible habit you are attempting to break away from when you leave them it is preferable to never return to it.

Throw away goods or love bombing trinkets: Gather up everything that reminds you of them and toss it all away. Delete anything that reminds you of them(like contacts, and images,) this would help you to move on.

Face the trauma: This may need either a person in your support network to be in contact with or a professional. To move on with your life, tossing the stuff of your narcissistic spouse is not enough. Face your trauma, quit being in denial, admit that what you went through is abuse. Cry over it but never return to such a relationship.

Document evidence: If a narcissist attempts to contact you again using another number, record each call, and screenshot each chat exchange to press charges if need be. Stalking is not simply criminal, it is an invasion of someone's privacy.

A Manual for Rebuilding Self-Esteem, Confidence, and Trust After a Narcissistic Relationship

Surviving a relationship with an egomaniac may have significant emotional effects. Rebuilding self-esteem, confidence, and trust is a vital milestone towards recovery. This book offers practical techniques to investigate the path of self-recuperation and build healthier partnerships in the wake of confronting the adverse repercussions of a narcissistic relationship.

Understanding Narcissistic Relationships:

Investigating the traits of a narcissistic relationship assists in spotting control, gaslighting, and emotional abuse. Recognizing these situations is the most crucial start toward recovery.

Rebuilding Self-Esteem and Confidence:

1)**Self-Compassion:** Self-compassion refers to treating yourself with kindness and understanding, recognizing any suffering you may be experiencing without criticizing yourself, and following a self-care routine to take care of yourself.

2. **Rediscovering interests and attributes:** Engaging in activities that bring joy and focusing on personal qualities can improve self-esteem.

3. **Positive Affirmations and Mindfulness:** Embracing affirmations and mindfulness approaches assists in reducing negative self-talk and being present at the moment.

Healing from Emotional Injury:

1. **Seeking Professional Assistance:** Treatment or coaching leads to overcoming mental harm and helps with establishing survival mechanisms.

2. **Journalling and Self-Reflection:** Communicating emotions via writing and reflecting about earlier interactions aids with emotional recovery.

Laying out Healthy Relationships and Trust:

1. **Recognizing Healthy Relationship Elements:** Learning the markers of good relationships — respect, mutual support, and communication — helps in recognizing healthy connections.

2. **Setting limits:** Laying up clear limits is crucial in sustaining good relationships and protecting personal well-being.

3. **Building Trust Continuously:** Getting some leeway to establish trust in new interactions and being transparent about prior experiences increases understanding and compassion.

Rehearsing Self-Care and Self-Validation:

1. **Prioritizing Self-Care:** Participating in exercises that preserve physical, emotional, and mental well-being is crucial.

2. **Approving Personal Worth:** Certifying one's value and appreciating personal accomplishments assists in improving self-worth.

Recuperation from a narcissistic relationship is a path that involves patience, self-compassion, and persistence. Rebuilding self-esteem, confidence, and trust entails accepting self-care works, seeking assistance, and step by step creating good connections. Keep in mind, mending takes time, however with responsibility, it's achievable to emerge more grounded and build a happy existence in the light of self-worth and good relationships.

Narcissistic abuse is more of mental abuse than physical abuse I can tell you for a fact that narcissistic abuse is more dangerous than physical abuse. Narcissistic abuse can make you question your sanity.

Narcissists target the inner you more than they target the outer you that is why is necessary you work on your inner self to heal from narcissistic abuse. As it has been said earlier on "When a narcissist can no longer control you, they tend to control how other people see you". A narcissist can even try to change the way the people around you see you that's how destructive they are.

Narcissistic relationships can cause mental health problems to You. They try to kill your self-esteem, they destroy your inner peace. They make you feel like you are not good at the things you do most of the time out of jealousy and also because they feel like nobody can do it better than they do. Dealing with a narcissist is traumatizing because while you are trying to build a relationship with your partner or you are even trying to build your partner, they aim to destroy you especially when you don't agree with them or you try to correct them and so you can only depend on them for validation.

the importance of sharing real-life stories for awareness, validation, and empowerment.

It is important to share your stories or views on narcissistic relationships either through social media or maybe with friends or family to prevent others from experiencing such things. while I was in a relationship with my narcissistic partner, I knew He was a narcissist through a movie that I saw but I didn't know much about narcissists, if I had known I would have left before He left me and I wouldn't feel this much pain. I got to know so much about narcissists after my relationship with him now it would prevent me from having a relationship with a narcissist again.

So it is really important to educate people about narcissistic relationships and how damaging they can be.

Maria's story began with the promise of a whirlwind romance that quickly turned into a storm of emotional manipulation and distress. She met a man named Alex, who initially appeared charming and confident. Maria soon fell deeply in love with him and their partnership seemed like a dream come true. However, it wasn't long before Maria found herself trapped in a maze of egotistical behavior.

Over time, Alex's charming facade began to crumble and he revealed himself to be someone who constantly sought affirmation and control. Maria felt the weight of his deceptive tactics, gaslighting, and emotional abuse. Her self-esteem gradually eroded as she tried to please him at the expense of her own needs and desires.

Maria reflects on her experience with pain, saying, "Nothing I did was ever enough. I was constantly bending over backwards for him, and his constant need for admiration left me feeling empty and unimportant."

Breaking free from this toxic relationship was a difficult and terrifying process for Maria. With the support of friends and a therapist, she learned to identify Alex's manipulative tactics and regained faith in her own existence. Setting boundaries and reclaiming her freedom were critical milestones in her journey towards healing.

"It wasn't easy," Maria admits, "but leaving that destructive cycle was the best decision I ever made. I rediscovered myself, regained my self-worth, and slowly began to heal."

Today, Maria is thriving and enjoying a life free from the constraints of a narcissistic relationship. Her story of self-discovery and resilience inspires others who may be facing similar struggles, encouraging them to break free and embark on their own journey towards recovery.

I would also like to share my story with You. I went through narcissistic abuse and I must tell you it wasn't easy. The reason why I accepted to date him was that I have never dated a GOD-fearing man, I needed a man that would bring me closer to God so I thought he was perfect, I accepted him thinking he was GOD fearing. I was aware that there is a difference between a GOD fearing man and a religious man.

We have different types of narcissists, we have the type that hides under religion pretending to be all good and holy. He was manipulative. He doesn't do anything for free, the time he helped my sister he charged her for it. He taught me not judge a book by its cover.

He was always talking about how he wanted to marry me, he wanted to trap me with a child.

One month into the relationship, he started to make me feel that he was doing me a favor by being in a relationship with me. He sexually assaulted me twice and pretended like it was a mistake I forgave him, and he blamed it on high level of testosterone.

I remember when I told him he was manipulative, he managed to turn everything around and make me feel like I was the manipulative one. He almost raised his hands on me. A lot of gaslighting that made me question my sanity. He ended the relationship with me because I forgot to wish his daughter Happy birthday on time, I explained why to him that day and I apologized but he still brought it up the next day, and I got angry. So he left me and never contacted me but guessed what I found peace without him in my life. Honestly, I couldn't believe it myself, I feel free now. I went with the no-contact rule, he can never contact me. It was not so easy but I needed to love myself more, I needed peace.

I cried, I prayed and built a support network, went to therapy now I feel better. I am more focused on myself and my career

Narcissistic abuse is a real one.

Although narcissistic abuse can be traumatizing, There are still some certain lesson that can sharpen your life from such experiences.

"I always say to myself in every bad situation there is always something good in it, sometimes a blessing and sometimes a lesson"

Self love: inadequate self love is what makes people settle for less, if you don't have proper self love for yourself that is when you accept people treating you like trash. No matter what never love anybody more than you love yourself. Remember to live yourself because if you don't you are just indirectly teaching people how to not love you

1. **Recognizing manipulative behaviors:** You can learn to identify manipulative tactics such as gaslighting, blame-shifting, and invalidation. This knowledge can help You in detecting similar behaviors in future relationships and avoiding them.

2. **Setting boundaries:** It is crucial to learn how to establish clear boundaries to protect Your well-being and prevent deception.

3. **Validating emotions and experiences:** It is important to acknowledge Your feelings and experiences and not let them be invalidated by the narcissist. This helps in recognizing the effects of gaslighting and paying more attention to Your inner sensations.

4. **Focusing on self-care and self-worth:** The experience helps in realize the importance of self-care and focusing on Your psychological and emotional welfare. This includes being kind to Yourself and rebuilding Your self-esteem and self-worth.

5. **Reclaiming autonomy and freedom:** You can learn to appreciate Your individuality and not depend on external validation.

6. **Recognizing healthy relationships**: Through the contrast with a narcissistic relationship, You can gain insights into what constitutes a healthy relationship.

7. **Empowerment through support networks:** You can learn the value of having a support system and seek connections with people who provide compassion, understanding, and comfort.

8. **Accepting imperfections:** It is important to recognize that everyone has flaws and that accepting them is necessary for personal growth.

9. **Growth and flexibility:** The experience can lead to Your personal growth and help in developing Your resilience and strength.

10. **Advocating for others:** The experience can empower You to share Your experiences, educate others, and campaign for awareness and support for people in similar situations.

These lessons can help in healing and empowering Yourself, leading to a more fulfilling life beyond the pain of narcissistic relationships.

Here is a complete analysis of tactics and coping processes commonly employed by survivors throughout recovery and mending from narcissistic relationships:

1. **No Contact or Restricted Contact:** Laying down no contact or restricted contact with the narcissistic person is a primary strategy. This restriction forestalls additional manipulation and emotional pain.

2. **Seeking Professional Help:** Engaging with experts, advisors, or care groups having some competence in recovery from narcissistic abuse gives a place of shelter for survivors to address emotions, obtain affirmation, and acquire direction.

3. **Training and Understanding:** Educating Yourself on narcissism, self-centeredness, emotional abuse, and manipulative methods is crucial. Understanding these views enables survivors to validate their experiences and recognize harmful relationship features.

4. **Self-Care and Health Works On:** Focusing on self-care is vital. Engaging in exercises that enhance mental, bodily, and emotional prosperity including meditation, exercise, leisure activities, and good eating upholds recovering.

5. **Defining and Implementing Limitations**: Figuring out how to lay out and keep up with appropriate limitations is a crucial coping method. Survivors differentiate and approve limitations to

shield themselves against future exploitation.

6. **Journaling and Self-Reflection:** Keeping a journal helps process emotions, chronicle interactions, and improve clarity. Self-reflection assists in understanding self-improvement, perceiving examples, and following development.

7. **Supportive Connections:** Developing connections with understanding and caring individuals delivers tremendous emotional aid. Healthy associations offer a sense of having a place and recognition.

8. **Practicing Mindfulness and Grounding Methods:** Mindfulness works on, breathing exercise, and grounding methods aid with supervising uneasiness and dissociation. These approaches aid in being present and controlling triggers.

9. **Gradual building of Self-esteem:** Engaging in affirmations, positive self-talk, and self-compassion techniques assists with repairing self-regard and self-worth injured by the narcissistic relationship.

10. **Engaging in Creative Outlets:** Exploring creative outlets like handiwork, music, composing, or other expressive activities fills in as a therapeutic release for emotions and assists in controlling trauma.

11. **Learning how to Trust Once More:** Continuously figuring out how to trust others and Yourself is a gradual but crucial stage. Building trust in good relationships helps with overcoming fear and restoring confidence.

12. **Obtaining Legal and Financial Counsel:** For individuals handling legal or financial repercussions due to the

connection, obtaining counsel from specialists assists in examining these details.

13. **Patience and Self-Compassion:** Acknowledging that healing is a continual cycle and it is necessary to exhibit moderation toward Yourself. Practicing self-compassion helps survivors to appreciate their experience without self-judgment.

By utilizing these tactics and coping mechanisms, you can investigate the obstacles of recovery, heal from the hurt of narcissistic relationships, and embark on a road towards self-improvement and strengthening.

For anyone currently facing or having gone through a narcissistic relationship, here is some encouragement and assistance to help you analyze the challenging conditions and aid in your recovery:

1. **Recognize the Red Flags:** Educate yourself about narcissistic traits and red flags in relationships. Familiarity with manipulation strategies assists in figuring out the dynamics at play.

2. **Focus on Your Well-Being:** Your psychological and personal wellness is crucial. Think about finding professional help from therapists, counselors, or support groups who have experience in dealing with narcissistic abuse.

3. **Define Your Limits:** Identify what you're comfortable with and what violates your boundaries. Communicate these limits to others.

4. **Set Boundaries and Cut Off Contact:** Establish clear boundaries or cut off contact with the narcissistic individual. Safeguard your fundamental well-being by keeping your distance whenever possible.

5. **Learn to Say No:** Don't be afraid to say no when something doesn't align with your boundaries or makes you uncomfortable. Your needs and feelings are valid.

6. **Practice Self-Care:** Prioritize self-care routines that enhance overall well-being. Participate in activities that bring you pleasure, relaxation, and fulfillment.

7. **Seek Support from Trusted People:** Surround yourself with understanding and

empathetic friends or family. Their support might bring affirmation and consolation during difficult moments.

8. **Trust Your Senses:** Trust your senses and believe your own reality. Gaslighting is a prevalent tactic in narcissistic relationships, and it's essential to trust yourself.

9. **Focus on Self-Improvement:** Use this experience as a time for self-reflection and growth. Consider writing to cope with your emotions and notice patterns. Consider the lessons learned and how they've helped you become a stronger person.

10. **Be Patient and Gentle with Yourself:** Recovery is a process that demands some commitment. Be patient and gentle with yourself as you explore healing and recreate your life. Practice self

compassion, Be kind to yourself throughout this recovery process. Acknowledge your feelings without judgment and show yourself compassion and understanding.

11. **Seek Legal and Financial Guidance:** If necessary, obtain legal or financial counsel to protect yourself from any legal or financial consequences of the partnership.

12. **Set Realistic Expectations:** Understand that the narcissistic person may not change. Embracing this reality helps in creating fair expectations for the future.

13. **Explore Your Interests and Hobbies:** Engage in activities that bring you joy and satisfaction to help you recover your individuality and interests.

14. **Forgive Yourself:** Don't blame yourself for the narcissistic person's

behavior. Understand that you are not responsible for their actions.

15. **Focus on Future Healthy Relationships:** Once you've recovered, focus on creating healthy relationships based on mutual respect, trust, and communication.

16. **Focus on Your Strengths:** Celebrate your accomplishments, no matter how small they may seem. They all contribute to your resilience.

17. **Embrace Self-Love:** Now is the best time to focus on yourself. Embracing self-love means understanding your inner value and accepting yourself fully, flaws and all. You are deserving of love, respect, and happiness, regardless of past experiences. Continuously remind yourself that you are beautiful.♥

18. **Moving On:** Moving on doesn't mean forgetting the past; it means reclaiming your life and embracing a more hopeful future.

19. **Seek Closure:** Closure doesn't always come from the other person; sometimes, it comes from within. Accepting what's happened for what it is can help you move forward and find closure.

Remember, healing from a narcissistic relationship is a gradual process. Seeking help, practicing self-care, and focusing on your well-being are key steps towards recovering your life and moving forward in a positive way. You have the right to live your life free from manipulation and abuse.

Exploring life after a narcissistic relationship may seem like an intimidating adventure, but it's important to remember that recovery is possible. The way forward begins with embracing self-love and creating healthy boundaries.

Breaking away from relationship that you thought was perfect is not easy. Thinking that you have finally found your dream partner and then getting your heart broken at the end of the day can be mentally exhausting. But take Marie for instance she went through all that toxicity and still emerged strong. If Marie can overcome all of these obstacles, you can do the same. Try to build your self-esteem, confidence, and love yourself more. Share your story to save other people from going through such abuse.

I want you to know that I see you, baby girl/boy. You are strong, powerful, and capable of overcoming any challenge and emerging even stronger. You are beautiful just the way you are, and you have so much to offer the world. Don't let anyone ever make you feel like you're not good enough.

In conclusion, navigating a narcissistic relationship is a tough and sometimes frightening process, leaving profound emotional scars and fractures that take time to repair. These relationships, marked by deception, emotional abuse, and a lack of empathy, severely damage people, reaching beyond the bounds of the relationship itself.

Survivors of narcissistic relationships undertake a difficult process of healing that entails regaining self-worth, establishing boundaries, and cultivating self-love. Through education, support networks, and self-reflection, people learn to spot red flags, validate their experiences, and prioritize their well-being.

The route to recovery from a narcissistic relationship is multidimensional. It requires embracing self-compassion, establishing clear limits, and eventually restoring sovereignty. Survivors create resilience, learning from their experiences and forging a route toward personal growth and strength.

Moving foward demands patience and self-acceptance. It entails recreating one's identity, rediscovering interests, and enjoying healthy relationships based on mutual respect and trust. While the wounds of a narcissistic relationship may endure, survivors emerge stronger, equipped with significant skills and insights that impact their future interactions and decisions.

Through self-love, setting boundaries, and a commitment to personal growth, survivors of narcissistic relationships embark on a journey toward a brighter, empowered future—a future characterized by resilience, self-assurance, and the ability to forge meaningful connections built on genuine empathy and understanding. Remember, your road toward recovery is genuine, and you deserve a life filled with love, respect, and satisfaction.